Who
ROCKED
the Boat?

Who
ROCKED
the Boat?

A Story about Navigating the
Inevitability of Change

By

CURTIS BATEMAN

CORAL GABLES

Copyright © 2022 by Franklin Covey Co.
Published by Mango Publishing, a division of Mango Publishing Group, Inc.

Cover Design: Carmen Fortunato
Book Design and Illustrations: Lauren Ball

For permission requests, please contact the publisher at:
Mango Publishing Group
2850 S Douglas Road, 4th Floor
Coral Gables, FL 33134 USA
info@mango.bz

For special orders, quantity sales, course adoptions and corporate sales, please email the publisher at sales@mango.bz. For trade and wholesale sales, please contact Ingram Publisher Services at customer.service@ingramcontent.com or +1.800.509.4887.

Who Rocked the Boat?: A Story about Navigating the Inevitability of Change

Library of Congress Cataloging-in-Publication number: 2022942976
ISBN: (print) 978-1-68481-077-2 (ebook) 978-1-68481-078-9
BISAC category code BUS046000, BUSINESS & ECONOMICS / Motivational

Printed in the United States of America

This book was made possible thanks to
the joint efforts of my friends and colleagues:
Marche Pleshette, Andy Cindrich, and Christi
Phillips, the co-authors of our upcoming book
Change: How to Turn Uncertainty into Opportunity
(to be released in Spring 2023).

Contents

Introduction

At FranklinCovey, we recognize the power of story to guide, instruct, and warn us along our individual journeys to greatness. This has been reaffirmed time and time again over four decades in business and 50 million books sold (and counting). We feel so strongly about the power of story that we consider it a leadership competency. The best of such stories, often short business parables by design, can bring to life a principle or practice so profound that it can change the trajectory of one's career, levels of contribution, legacy, or even the organization itself.

What follows is a short story about a boat and its crew along a fantastical journey—one that forces them to adapt and ultimately thrive through disruptive change. I've chosen the business story format as a way of inviting you as the reader to become a co-owner of the story with me—reflect on your experiences with change alongside those of our imaginary captain and crew. I've learned the power of shared stories from my time spent with Spencer Johnson during the *Who Moved My Cheese?* phenomenon. This was the beginning of my work to expand the narrative on the topic of change: personal, professional, self-initiated, or unexpected. To long-standing FranklinCovey readers, I'd challenge you to put aside what you might typically expect from an organizational and personal change book and instead take a ride on this narrative journey. As you do, reflect on your own experiences with change.

The great insight that came to me and my partner after years of working on real-world change initiatives was that as messy and chaotic as change often feels, it moves through a predictable pattern, and that pattern serves as the undergirding of this story. If you're leading a team, leading an organization, parenting, coaching, volunteering, or looking to enact a meaningful change in your life, this book was written for you. And it comes with a promise: the fantastical adventure of our captain and crew will serve as a map for understanding not only how we (and those around us) often react to change, but how taking ownership at the right moment can inspire new strategies, opportunities, and even greater results.

The somewhat ironic title of *Who Rocked the Boat?* shouldn't be interpreted as a prescription for uncovering who's to blame for an unwanted change. Rather, it's an acknowledgement of how we often first react to unexpected change—who can I blame for this?! A more accurate but less catchy title for this book could be, *Okay, Since I'm in This Change Boat With Some Other Folks and We're All Holding Oars, Maybe We Should Look at Our Map and Then Work Together to Paddle Our Way Out of This?* You get the idea. This is a book that begins with a fundamental acknowledgement: change success isn't simply a rigidly followed process or communication plan; it's first about people. Not pointing a finger at someone to blame them personally for a disruption, but understanding how we and others tend to react to change and marshalling that into a strategy for effectively moving forward. Allow me to use the people theme as an entry point into the story. Consider a text exchange between a leader facing an unwanted change and someone they trust...

*A Leader's
Dilemma...*

Tuesday, 10:41

Help!

Company just announced a BIG change. My team's right in the middle of it all. Yikes!

I've never led a team through this kind of a thing before :(

Tuesday, 10:50

What do I do?

Where do I start?

Breathe... You've got this

Tuesday, 11:23

Easy for you to say! I am so overwhelmed

I'm glad you messaged. This is why you asked me to be your mentor. Moments like this, right?

Right

Advice

I just sent you a whimsical story about change. Read it then text me when you're done

PART ONE

The River
"Routine"

There once was a captain and crew who set off in their fanciful ship, *Results*. They had been tasked with delivering their cargo past the mountain where their port of call awaited. The crew was content, perhaps even a little bored, as *Results* moved at a slow but predictable pace. Everyone expected a smooth journey—the waterway was gentle, the scenery pleasant, and the skies clear and comforting.

The crew had worked together for some time and knew each other well. *Move* was the engineer who kept their steam engine stoked and running. *Minimize* served as the chief mate and oversaw the cargo. *Resist*, the second mate, was responsible for ship and crew safety. *Wait* was a deckhand who did a little bit of everything. And finally *Quits* and *Quit* were twins who took turns piloting the ship down the river. They all served under the captain, who was responsible for everything related to *Results* and her crew.

"I prefer gentle rivers like this one," *Wait* said to the others.

"They make for an easy trip," *Minimize* added.

"And it does give us time to run some drills," *Move* said, always an endless fountain of energy. "You know, sharpen our skills and learn something new!"

Resist raised an eyebrow in response. "Do more work for the same pay? Yeah, I'll take a pass."

"Same here," *Quits* called down from the helm. "Don't stress yourselves out—this trip will be as smooth as silk."

"True," *Quit* agreed. "Smooth as silk when I'm at the helm!" They all laughed at *Quit's* over-confidence.

But river journeys, like life, often unfold in surprising ways.

In the distance, the sound of a muffled roar rose above the chug of *Result's* steam-powered engines. Noticing the river moving faster and faster, the captain knew what it likely meant: waterfall ahead! But before they could swing the boat around, the swift current pulled them into a rushing, churning rapid.

"All hands, man the boat!" the captain exclaimed, issuing the traditional order for the crew to don their life jackets and prepare for the unknown. "Waterfall ahead!"

But not every crew member reacted in the same way.

Move, who loved the excitement of a new adventure, grabbed a shovel and began heaping coal into the boilers. "The quicker we get to the waterfall, the more exciting—and fast—our trip will be!" *Move* loved to race ahead and embrace the thrill of the ride.

Minimize, who wanted to know only what was expected and to do as little as possible, was cautious not to overthink or expend more energy than necessary: "Is it *really* a waterfall? Let's not be doing any more than we have to," said *Minimize*, looking up from reviewing the cargo manifest.

Wait noted the captain's warning but remained in place. "I've been fooled by such noises before. Best to hold off and see what happens," *Wait* said, monitoring the rest of the crew and watching how they reacted before making a move.

Resist believed they should refuse to go further—a waterfall could easily destroy *Results*. *Resist* shouted to the others, "We must fight against the pull of the current! Help me throw the anchor overboard!" But the captain intervened—they were moving too fast, and if the anchor caught, it would capsize the ship.

Quits and *Quit* had other ideas. *Quits*, thinking the jungle a better alternative to the waterfall, shouted: "Good luck to you, but I'm outta here!" Then *Quits* jumped overboard and swam for shore.

Quit, on the other hand, wanted out but wasn't ready to abandon the ship or crew just yet. After all, who knew if the jungle was any less dangerous than the waterfall? So *Quit* stepped away from the helm, grabbed the rail, and said, "No use steering now."

The captain grabbed the wheel and guided *Results* toward the precipice ahead.

PART TWO

Down the Waterfall

The ship bounced and listed as it neared the crest of the waterfall. Awash in the roar of the falls, the spray of the water, and the rush of the wind, the crew was gripped by an onslaught of emotions as they plummeted.

"I told you this would happen! We're goners!" *Quit* shouted above the fray.

"We should have dropped the anchor!" *Resist* exclaimed.

"Oh my!" *Wait* cried out, clinging to the rails and terrified of how much worse things could get.

Move whooped with delight and relished the adrenaline rush.

Minimize kept quiet.

The captain knew they were in the thick of it and seeing emotions running high, thought, *How do I help the crew after we hit bottom?*

With a tremendous splash, *Results* plunged into the pool beneath the waterfall. The engines belched hot steam and shrieked in protest as the crew crashed and tumbled into each other. Several of the crew fell overboard, and others had to scramble to toss life preservers and pull them in. *Wait* was even forced beneath the water by the pressure of the falls but managed to swim back to the surface and be rescued. Drenched, battered, and hurting, the crew went on to assess the damage. *Results* had taken a significant beating, but the ship remained afloat as they drifted in the water's current.

"So now what?" *Resist* asked, prepared to oppose anything else that was new and unexpected.

Wait watched the others, looking for a clue as to what to do.

After assessing the ship's damage, the captain said, "The waterfall wreaked havoc on our poor ship and left us bruised and broken, and now we need to work together to get back on course."

"But why did we have to take *this* route?" *Quit* moaned. "There are lots of other waterways out there. Whose crazy idea was it to take the river with the waterfall?"

The captain replied, "If we were to always take the same rivers in the same ways, we'd never find faster and better routes. No river will ever stay constant, so waterfalls will always be a part of the journey."

"So what now?" *Resist* challenged.

The captain offered a reassuring smile. "I know this is not what any of us expected, but we'll figure it out together."

"Couldn't agree more, cap'," *Move* said enthusiastically. "Trying new things makes life more interesting."

"I don't need a more interesting life," *Resist* grumbled.

"For the record, I wanted none of this," *Quit* said.

The current carried *Results* to a sandy beach where they dropped anchor and disembarked. As they gathered on the shore, they noticed how the sand pulled and tugged at their boots. It was slow moving here, as if the place wanted to keep them stuck. The captain said, "I think we can rest here for a bit, but we don't want to stay too long. Let's decide what to do and get moving."

"As long as we don't spend too much time talking," *Move* said, shifting from foot to foot.

"Let's just find where the river picks up again *down here*," *Minimize* suggested.

"But that won't lead us to where we need to go," the captain replied. "Our charge is to take *Results* and her cargo to the mountains and port beyond—both of which are on higher ground."

"Well, the cargo can spoil for all I care," *Quit* said. "I hate it here."

"We still have a job to do," the captain said, looking

up at the cliff. "That *hasn't* changed and getting to the top seems our best option."

"Okay then, sure...we'll just *magically* sail our ship up a vertical rock wall," *Resist* said sarcastically. *Resist* knew that sometimes the best way to stop an idea was to mock it.

Frustrated, the crew scattered to different points along the beach, lost in their own thoughts about what they were willing and wanting to do.

The captain approached *Wait,* who was sitting on a boulder. "Mind if I ask you something?"

Wait shrugged.

"Why is the team so hesitant to go up the cliff?" the captain asked.

"Well, I'd say the crew doesn't want to rush into anything."

The captain considered that for a moment and then asked, "Do you think that's true for everyone, or is it just how you're feeling?"

"Well, I know I feel that way. Plus, I've been through this kind of thing before, and it never works out. People can talk all the big ideas they like, but in the end, everyone just does their own thing."

Understanding *Wait's* concerns, the captain then had similar discussions with each crew member. In the end, everyone had their own concerns and reactions, but what the crew mostly wanted was a clear, well-thought-out, and well-communicated plan that wouldn't end up being a waste of time. Following some intense brainstorming and discussion, the captain shared a proposal: "I think we should take the ship apart—"

"Hold on," *Resist* interrupted. "You're suggesting we take the *entire* ship apart? And then what...? Carry it up bit by bit? On our backs? That's the worst idea ever, cap'. And no one here will ever support it."

But *Minimize* saw it differently. "It's really not such a big deal. We can construct a hoist using our pulleys, mast, and rigging, and then pull *Results* up piece by piece. Better than on our backs, for sure. Of course, I'm not saying I *want* to go up the cliff, but if that's the plan, we can at least be smart about it."

"I love it!" *Move* exclaimed, to no one's surprise whatsoever.

"Have you forgotten how *much* it all weighs?" *Quit* asked. "Even if we break *Results* down to her smallest parts. I don't care how many pulleys we have; we'll never be able to do it." *Quit* then turned to *Resist*. "You're with me on this, right?"

Resist nodded with a dodgy grin.

"Okay," said the captain, "but what's the alternative?"

The crew glanced at each other. They couldn't think of a better way to get the ship and its cargo to the top.

The captain said, "Alright then. Let's get started."

The others nodded in agreement, some less enthusiastically than others. But it was enough for *Wait* to see things were happening. "I'll help you get the tools," *Wait* called out to *Move*, who had already taken off toward the ship.

The captain was pleased they had decided to get

to work and knew getting out of the ravine would stretch the crew in ways they weren't used to.

PART THREE

Up the Other Side

Thehe plan they came up with required several steps. First, they would break the ship down into manageable pieces. Next, they'd build ladders and scale the rock face, carrying the parts necessary to construct the winch at the top. Then they'd use the winch to hoist the bundles and cargo. Finally, with everything and everyone safely gathered on the plateau above, they'd reassemble *Results* and put the ship into the river system—getting back to things just as they were before.

Everyone felt it was a solid plan, save for *Move*,

who had left midway through the discussion and scaled a third of the cliff. *Move* had coils of rope, several pulleys, and an assortment of tools stuffed into a utility belt. The captain had to call *Move* back, who frowned but began the descent.

"You do realize we still need all that stuff down here!" *Minimize* shouted at *Move*, just so the point wasn't lost.

With *Move* back on the beach, the crew went about disassembling the ship, breaking down the steam-powered engine, unloading the cargo, unstitching and folding the canopy and emergency sails, coiling the ropes, securing the heavy pulley, and cutting the jiggermast to use as the arm for the winch. Whenever a particular task felt daunting, *Minimize* reminded them they'd all been trained on ship repairs, so taking *Results* apart wasn't such a lofty endeavor. Eventually the crew completed the breakdown of the ship, gathered the materials for the platforms, and built the required ladders.

Now it was time to climb.

But even *Minimize* had underestimated the required effort. It was extremely hard work. They had to find a suitable spot on the rock wall, hold the ladder in place, climb, secure it, build a small platform, then hand the next ladder up, repeating the process over and over. Sometimes the crew came to spots where they couldn't find any good places to fasten the ladder and had to back down and try a different route. Sometimes they had to lay the ladder sideways and travel in a direction they didn't want to go, hoping to find another way up. Other times, the wind threatened to blow them off the cliff! These and many more challenges had to be overcome as the crew zigzagged across the cliff's face, sometimes moving up, sometimes moving sideways, and sometimes moving down; but eventually and persistently, they continued the ascent.

Finally, they made it to the top. There, they constructed the pulley as those below secured and hoisted the materials upward.

Success! Or so they thought.

It turned out, much to their dismay, that *Quit* had been right all along. The parts were too heavy, even with all their pulleys and the mast for support! Try as they might, the crew just couldn't muster enough strength to pull the heavy bundles up.

"You know that part of a story when you get to

say, 'I told you so'?" *Quit* announced to the group.

"Please don't," *Wait* implored.

"Well, that was a waste," *Minimize* said, looking at the winch they had constructed.

"Couldn't disagree more," *Move* said. "We deserve some kudos for making it this far."

"Okay," *Resist* said. "Go ahead and give yourself a pat on the back. Feel better now?"

"*Move* does have a point," the captain said, knowing just how hard the crew had worked to get to where they were. "We solved all kinds of challenges on the cliff."

As the crew reflected on how hard they had worked, it did feel as if they had become better at figuring out how to overcome the unexpected.

"Remember when we were running low on bolts?"

Wait asked. "We found a way to use the rock crevices as natural anchors."

"Or when the rock face jutted out and the ladders wouldn't work," *Move* said. "*Resist* made a *rope* ladder using a bunch of clever clove-hitch knots."

"It was the most efficient solution," *Resist* said.

Realizing all they had accomplished and with the captain's encouragement to try again, the crew shifted from complaining to solving the problem in front of them. Eventually, they decided they could repurpose the boilers and transform their people-powered winch into a steam-powered one. The boiler parts were big but not so heavy that the crew couldn't lift them on their own. That meant they could use their existing pulleys to get them to the top.

When they had finished hoisting the boiler parts,

Move reassembled the components and adapted the steam engine to the new task.

When it was done, and the fire lit and stoked, the crew stood back and watched. Suddenly the piston began to move, then began pumping as the exhaust hiccuped puffs of steam. *Minimize* pulled the lever and their new, mechanical winch turned with ease.

The crew shouted in celebration, giving each other high-fives. The captain smiled, noting it had been some time since they had had a win like that. A very long time, in fact.

When all the ship's heavy cargo and large pieces were out of the ravine, the crew made their last climb, retrieving their ladders and platforms as they scrambled to the top. Up and down, over and over. Scaling the cliff had turned out to be even harder than the captain had predicted. But as long as the crew had worked together, step by step and foot by foot, they had gotten themselves out.

From their new vantage point, the captain and crew could see the waterfall and river that marked the beginning of their journey. And across the grassy highlands, they caught sight of a river leading to the mountains. Everyone was exhausted but proud of their accomplishment—soon they'd be back to the way things were!

PART FOUR

The Sky's the Limit

B ut something was different.

The crew had changed. They began to celebrate.

"Say what you will, but we've overcome a lot to get to this point," the captain said. "And hey, it took everyone working together."

The captain then turned to each of the crewmembers in turn: "*Move*, you're never stuck in the old way of doing things. I can always count on you to try something new. And *Minimize*, I love how you always focus on what's necessary, so we don't get in over our heads. *Wait*, you ask the best questions, and you don't rush headlong into things. *Resist*, you force us to test our thinking, which is invaluable. And *Quit*, even when you're disengaged, I've learned you can be an early warning signal to something the rest of us may not be seeing. What an amazing crew you are! It's great to be back on track, but we sure lost a lot of time."

Minimize said, "I don't want to be away from home any longer than we have to. Makes me wonder what *else* we could do to speed things up."

"That's an interesting thought," *Move* said.

"Maybe we should come up with some ideas," *Wait* suggested. "Like reassemble *Results* so it cuts through the water faster."

"Or leave some of the unnecessary cargo behind,"

Quit suggested, liking the idea of not having to move everything back to the vessel.

Move added, "I bet I could get more power out of the engines if I modified them more."

"A faster ship on a winding river is a terrible idea," *Resist* said, suspicious of any change that came with an overabundance of enthusiasm.

"I love the creativity," the captain said, "but *Resist* has a point—the river has some natural limitations. I wonder if there's a way to get *off* the river...?"

"What about a steam-powered walking machine?" *Move* suggested, liking the idea of stomping around in a giant mechanical rig.

"*Stepping* off a waterfall? Should I take the rest of the day to explain what a horrible idea *that* is?" *Resist* asked. "Because I could."

"Well, I don't see how *stepping* off a waterfall is any better than *floating* off of one," *Wait* replied.

"Wait a minute," *Resist* said flatly, "let's not get crazy. We're a *ship's* crew. That's what we know, and that's what we should return to."

"But there are different kinds of ships, aren't there?" *Move* said. "Different ships do different things and solve different problems."

Wait considered the idea for a moment then exclaimed, "Like *air*ships!"

The captain could suddenly see it and turned to the parts spread across the grass in ordered piles. "An *air*ship... it's not so impossible when you think about it. Same basic build, just some modifications to get us off the ground. Just think of it...in an airship, we could sail above the rivers and jungle at great speed—*Results* would literally rise!"

Minimize could envision it as well. "Still a ship, sure, but changed just enough to make it better. The canopy could be stitched into a balloon."

"Fine...it's a big modification, but it's not impossible. We have plenty of material, especially with the emergency sails."

"And the steam from the boilers could heat the air and give us lift," *Move* said. "We'd need a good deal for all the cargo, but those engines run hot."

"And the propeller could turn like before, only now in the air instead of the water!" *Wait* exclaimed. "Same basic mechanism as before."

"You'd need a helmsman to steer her," *Quit* said. "But that feels close enough to my job as before. Just...higher."

With renewed energy, the crew went to work turning their idea into a reality.

Sometime later, as the sun rested on the horizon, a new airship took shape. With its canopy and sails refashioned, boilers repurposed, and propellers realigned, the vessel rose into the air. The rudders, now serving as fins, turned as *Quit* spun the helm. The airship gracefully pivoted toward the mountains, the direction of their port of call. No longer were the captain and crew subject to the slow and meandering rivers that stretched out beneath them.

In the distance, the crew caught sight of *Quits*, who stood at the edge of the jungle and waved in astonishment. They could only hope *Quits*' next adventure would be as rewarding as theirs. But for them, in their new airship, the captain and crew steamed ahead with greater speed and efficiency than before. There would be challenges to come, of course, but those were for another time. Besides, the crew had learned they were more resilient and innovative than they had previously believed. And so in this moment, they celebrated the fact that where *Results* had once moved along a slow and mostly predictable path, she now soared.

As did they.

Wow. That waterfall
is totally my life
right now!! So many
thoughts...

Where should I start?
I have a gazillion
questions

Easy! :)
Share the story with
your team. Ask them to
read it.

I'll send some
conversation starters.
Pick some and start
talking with your team

Thanks! That was fast

That will get you started.

Lunch tomorrow? We can talk about how it went. Next steps.

Sounds great. I'll review what you sent and we can talk then. And seriously, thanks!

Change
Conversation
Starters

Who Rocked the Boat? was written to be used in a variety of settings and as a springboard for discussion and reflection. Use the prompts below to further explore individual (personal), coaching (one-on-one), and/or team/organizational changes:

PERSONAL CHANGE (SELF-REFLECTION QUESTIONS)

- Did you put your boat in this river, or did an external circumstance put your boat in this river? How do you feel about that?

- When you look at the cliff on the other side of the waterfall, what does your change look like at the top of the cliff? How clear is that vision? Can you describe it to someone else?

- Is that vision enough to motivate you after the waterfall and to get up the cliff? If not, does your vision need work? Do you need more skills or resources?

- Share the vision with someone else. Ask them what would make the story better.

- What other information will you need to choose the cliff versus floating further down the river ravine?

COACHING (ONE-ON-ONE)

- Using the river journey, tell me about your change.

- Which reaction most closely matches yours?

- Are you comfortable with your reaction? Is it the right one for this change?

- What part of our "change river journey" are you most comfortable with? Least? Why?

- On the beach, the captain had a conversation with each member of the crew. If that were you on the beach, what would have been your concerns? What questions should the captain have asked you? How would you have answered?

TEAM/ORGANIZATIONAL CHANGE

- What is our river routine? Who can share our status quo? What about it feels stagnant? Where does it feel safe and predictable? Where is it tired and uninspiring? Do those answers line up with the "why we are changing" message from the business? Should they? If they don't, who can you talk to, so you can understand why they don't?

- Who in our organization is in the good ship *Results* and will be experiencing the change? Who is back at the corporate office and not experiencing the change? Should any of those people be in the boat because they can help with the journey up the cliff?

- Using the illustration of the river journey— place each team in the organization where they are on the river journey. Should each team's boat be in the same place? Why? Why not?

- Does your team's good ship *Results* have all the resources on the boat you might need for climbing your cliff? What other resources might the organization load in your boat?

- Is your ship's captain more informed about the journey than you, or do you have about the same amount of information? If you were to help your captain, what other information would you hope the captain has about the journey? Come up with your best five questions for the captain to discover what would help your team be successful with the journey over the falls and back up the cliff.

Who Rocked the Boat? Reflection

W e all travel along various rivers in life, which means that at any moment we can find ourselves navigating their uncertainty—whether from a global pandemic, a shift in employment, a new role on a team, starting a new course in school, the birth of a child, the death of a loved one, a divorce, or responding to a setback on a project or personal goal. In the story, you've been introduced to a predictable pattern of change and the Five Common Reactions to Change. Consider how the experiences of the captain and crew coincide or differ from *your experiences with change*. Then answer the questions on the next few pages:

- What insights or "ahas" about change did you have while reading or listening to the story?

- Which of the characters have you observed or

identified with in your own change reaction or the reaction of others: *Move, Minimize, Wait, Resist, Quit/Quits?*

- Could you empathize with some of the characters more than others? Who felt most like *you?*

- How did the relationships between people come to make the change successful (or ultimately undermine its success)?

- How did those in your boat who expressed different reactions to change come to contribute to the change? Was this because of their different reactions?

- Reactions to change can extend beyond the five characters in the story. Who else was on *your* boat when going through a difficult change? (Ex. *Revolt*, who's ready to grab a torch and metaphorically burn the initiative to the ground; *Fear*, who is gripped by negative thinking and dread and will share it at every opportunity; *Ambivalence*, who is uncertain or unable to decide what course to follow; etc.)

Even though change may feel chaotic and unsettling, it follows a predictable pattern. Consider how you moved through your own change journey:

- The routine of the *status quo* of the river at the beginning.
  - ◇ What did this stage feel like for you? Contemplate the emotions and inter-actions going on.
- The *disruption* and chaos of the waterfall.
  - ◇ How large was the waterfall you went over?
  - ◇ What did it feel like while going through it?

- ✧ How did those with you behave?

- The need to *adopt* new strategies to scale the cliff and carry *Results* back to where they were.

  - ✧ After the waterfall, how difficult or easy was it to reach a decision to move forward? How many times did you have to find a new route, hit a dead end, or start over? How well-thought-out was your plan, or was it mostly *ad hoc* as you made your climb? If you were relying on others, how did they make the ascent easier or harder?

  - ✧ As you ascend the next change cliff, what can you and your team do that plants the seeds for future innovation?

- The *innovation* that results from leveraging the struggle and learnings from climbing up the cliff into new ways of thinking and doing.

✧ In the end, the crew re-invents the good ship *Results* as an airship. What does this leap from a *water* ship to an *air* ship suggest about the possible innovation connected to a change? Does the innovative creativity need to *always* produce this much of a transformative leap, or can it come in smaller degrees? Why or why not?

✧ Did you leverage the experience of change into doing *more* than getting back to the way things were before? What kinds of innovations sprang from the experience?

Some waterfalls are unforeseen; others are planned.

● Is the change experience different based on whether you charted a course knowing a waterfall was ahead or stumbled into one by accident? Why or why not?

Most ships come with a captain.

- How did the captain reflect the role a leader played in your change initiative, for good or for bad?

- What could the leader have done differently to help the "crew" thrive or simply survive the experience?

How might you use the story to introduce and talk about change with others?

The Change Process Is Not a Mystery

T he story illustrates a familiar pattern that we have seen in working with countless organizations and individuals. In the next few pages, we will take ideas from the story and connect them to the Change Model. But first, three important change principles:

- **Change is not a mystery**. It follows a predictable pattern we can take advantage of. We call this pattern the Change Model.

- **There are five common reactions to change**. There are not "right" or "wrong" reactions, but warrant understanding and reflecting given whatever change we're facing.

- **The leader/captain** (whether a formal leader or one's own best instincts around change) **can make or break a change's success** based on the skills they employ and are willing to learn.

One of the additional lessons of the story is that without change, we don't progress. And while change is a constant and driving force, it doesn't have to be a mystery. The more familiar you become with both the reactions to change and the Change Model, the more effectively you can preempt fear and turn the uncertainty of change into a meaningful opportunity.

THE FIVE COMMON REACTIONS TO CHANGE

We all experience change differently, but the story highlights five common reactions:

- MOVE: has an impulse to charge into action toward a change

- MINIMIZE: focuses on what's expected and changes as little as possible

- WAIT: doesn't act immediately; slowly adapts when they see others changing

- RESIST: dislikes the change and tries to convince others to fight it, privately or publicly

- QUIT: opts out and either leaves (a team, a relationship, etc.) or stays but refuses to engage with the change

The Leader (Captain)

For the captain/leader, it may be tempting to view change as a process to be rigidly followed, marching people through it as efficiently as possible. But that's not the right focus. Change is about people first—whether leading yourself through one or more of the reactions to formally leading a team through a change and toward a goal.

The Change Model

Who Rocked the Boat? is a story about the nature of change. It's a way for organizations, teams, and individuals to talk about how they experience change.

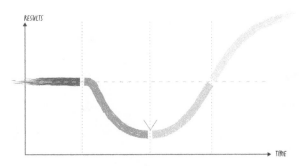

The story describes the predictable pattern for change. The Change Model provides the structure necessary to orient oneself as to where you are in a given change and gain clarity about what's ahead. Like the ship's crew, you can use the Change Model as a map to chart your way forward: making key decisions, adopting new behaviors, and building the conditions for innovation to take hold.

The Four Zones

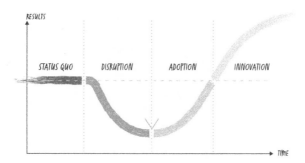

There are four zones in the Change Model:

- The Zone of Status Quo

- The Zone of Disruption

- The Zone of Adoption; and

- The Zone of Innovation.

ZONE OF STATUS QUO

The Zone of Status Quo is what you experience before a change is introduced. Here you generally feel comfortable as you and those with you accept business as usual, even if it's just the calm before the storm. This is the zone where those who are the most successful at change invest their time and energy to prepare for what's ahead.

ZONE OF DISRUPTION

As you plummet over the edge of the change waterfall, you enter the Zone of Disruption. Like the crew in our story, it's easy to find yourself awash in chaos and ambiguity as results take a nosedive. Many of the things you were used to having can disappear and what you were used to doing often stops working.

The Zone of Disruption feels uncomfortable at best and miserable at worst. With emotions running high, those in the Zone of Disruption often default to three questions:

- *What's* changing?
- *Why* is it changing?
- *How* will it affect me?

ZONE OF ADOPTION

Here you must adjust to the new reality of change. Because of this, the Zone of Adoption is where most change efforts fail. Like the crew aboard the good ship *Results*, you're unlikely to climb your way out on your first attempt. Ascending the Zone of Adoption means trying new things even if the efforts end in failure. You may feel like you're making progress for a bit, then suddenly find yourself sliding backwards. That's all part of the journey in the Zone of Adoption. The secret is to keep moving and building the change muscle that will not only empower you to get to your previous results but set the stage for something more.

Zone of Innovation

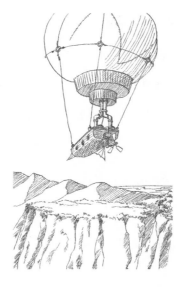

In the Zone of Innovation you've not only reclaimed the results from before the waterfall but are poised to push them even higher. Making it to the Zone of Innovation means you have developed the change muscle necessary to do more than arrive at where you started—you've learned to adapt and overcome traditional thinking and challenges in ways that can still be beneficial. Sadly, those who fall short of the Zone of Innovation have paid the cost for change without reaping all the benefits.

In the Zone of Innovation, you have the chance to put your new change muscle to work, asking questions like:

- *What are the possibilities?*
- *What haven't we thought of before?*
- *How can we make things even better?*

Conclusion

Now you too know the story of Who Rocked the Boat. Tell it, share it, use it. Look at your reaction to the next change you encounter: recognize it, decide if it is the right reaction, choose how you will respond. Help yourself and others along the journey to greatness.

Curtis Bateman is one of FranklinCovey's lead change experts and the author of *Who Rocked the Boat: A Story about Navigating the Inevitability of Change*. He currently serves as the Vice President, International Direct Offices and as a Senior Change Consultant. Curtis's experience spans 25 years with a diversity of experience across the globe and contributes to the international success of FranklinCovey's global divisions. He is an internationally recognized presenter, content developer, and business leader and coach.

Prior to FranklinCovey, Curtis was President and CEO of Red Tree Leadership, where he took the company from a single product to a suite of change and leadership solutions. Among these solutions he was a co-contributor to the development of five new training programs focused on change in the workplace and in life.

Curtis currently resides in Utah with his wife and four children, where he spends time enjoying the outdoors through hiking and photography.

FranklinCovey

FranklinCovey is the most trusted leadership company in the world, with operations in over 160 countries. We transform organizations by partnering with our clients to build leaders, teams, and cultures that get breakthrough results through collective action, which leads to a more engaging work experience for their people.

Available through the FranklinCovey All Access Pass®, our best-in-class content, solutions, experts, technology, and metrics seamlessly integrate to ensure lasting behavior change at scale.

This approach to leadership and organizational change has been tested and refined by working with tens of thousands of teams and organizations over the past 30 years.

To learn more, visit
FRANKLINCOVEY.COM.

FranklinCovey
All Access Pass

The FranklinCovey All Access Pass® provides unlimited access to our best-in-class content and solutions, allowing you to expand your reach, achieve your business objectives, and sustainably impact performance across your organization.

AS A PASSHOLDER, YOU CAN:

- Access FranklinCovey's world-class content, whenever and wherever you need it, including *The 7 Habits of Highly Effective People®: Signature Edition 4.0*, Leading at the *Speed of Trust®*, *The 5 Choices to Extraordinary Productivity®*, and *Unconscious Bias: Understanding Bias to Unleash Potential™*.

- Certify your internal facilitators to teach our content, deploy FranklinCovey consultants, or use digital content to reach your learners with the behavior-changing content you require.

- Have access to a certified implementation specialist who will help design Impact Journeys for behavior change.

- Organize FranklinCovey content around your specific business-related needs.

- Build a common learning experience throughout your entire global organization with our core-content areas localized into 23 languages.

Join thousands of organizations using the All Access Pass to implement strategy, close operational gaps, increase sales, drive customer loyalty, and improve employee engagement.

To learn more, visit
FRANKLINCOVEY.COM or call **1-888-868-1776**.

FranklinCovey

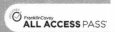

CHANGE
How to Turn Uncertainty Into Opportunity™

Change happens all the time, whether we choose it or it chooses us.

Yet, when faced with change, many organizations primarily focus on the process. Successful change takes more than that—**it's your people who make change happen**. And as people, we're wired to react to change to survive, which can make change feel difficult or threatening. Successful leaders engage their people in change, making it feel less uncertain and more like an opportunity.

Introducing *Change: How to Turn Uncertainty Into Opportunity*

When we recognize that change follows a predictable pattern, we can learn to manage our reactions and understand how to navigate change, both functionally and emotionally. This allows us to consciously determine how to best move forward—even in the most challenging stages.

Change: How to Turn Uncertainty Into Opportunity helps individuals and leaders learn how to successfully navigate any workplace change to improve results.

To learn more about how FranklinCovey's
Change: How to Turn Uncertainty Into Opportunity
can support your team and organization, visit

franklincovey.com/leadership/navigate-change

Read More
FROM THE FRANKLINCOVEY LIBRARY

  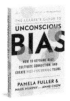

MORE THAN 50 MILLION COPIES SOLD

Learn more about how to develop yourself personally, lead your team,
or transform your organization with these bestselling books, by visiting
7habitsstore.com.

 FranklinCovey

FRANKLINCOVEY
ON LEADERSHIP

WITH
SCOTT MILLER

Join *On Leadership* host Scott Miller for
weekly interviews with thought leaders,
bestselling authors, and world-renowned
experts on the topics of organizational culture,
leadership development, execution,
and personal productivity.

FEATURED INTERVIEWS INCLUDE:

CHRIS McCHESNEY
THE 4 DISCIPLINES OF
EXECUTION

SUSAN DAVID
EMOTIONAL AGILITY

KIM SCOTT
RADICAL CANDOR

DANIEL PINK
WHEN

SETH GODIN
THE DIP, LINCHPIN, PURPLE COW

NELY GALÁN
SELF MADE

LIZ WISEMAN
MULTIPLIERS / IMPACT PLAYERS

GUY KAWASAKI
WISE GUY

STEPHEN M. R. COVEY
THE SPEED OF TRUST

ARIANNA HUFFINGTON
THRIVE NOW

NANCY DUARTE
DATA STORY, SLIDE:OLOGY

STEPHANIE McMAHON
CEO, WWE

DEEPAK CHOPRA
ABUNDANCE

ANNE CHOW
CEO, AT&T BUSINESS

GENERAL STANLEY
McCHRYSTAL
LEADERS: MYTH AND REALITY

MATTHEW
McCONAUGHEY
GREENLIGHTS

Subscribe to FranklinCovey's *On Leadership*
to receive weekly videos, tools, articles,
and podcasts at

FRANKLINCOVEY.COM/ONLEADERSHIP.

Mango Publishing, established in 2014, publishes an eclectic list of books by diverse authors—both new and established voices—on topics ranging from business, personal growth, women's empowerment, LGBTQ+ studies, health, and spirituality to history, popular culture, time management, decluttering, lifestyle, mental wellness, aging, and sustainable living. We were recently named 2019 *and* 2020's #1 fastest-growing independent publisher by *Publishers Weekly*. Our success is driven by our main goal, which is to publish high-quality books that will entertain readers as well as make a positive difference in their lives.

Our readers are our most important resource; we value your input, suggestions, and ideas. We'd love to hear from you—after all, we are publishing books for you!

Please stay in touch with us and follow us at:
    Facebook: Mango Publishing
    Twitter: @MangoPublishing
    Instagram: @MangoPublishing
    LinkedIn: Mango Publishing
    Pinterest: Mango Publishing
    Newsletter: mangopublishinggroup.com/newsletter

Join us on Mango's journey to reinvent publishing, one book at a time.

CPSIA information can be obtained
at www.ICGtesting.com
Printed in the USA
LVHW111506070223
738880LV00007B/523